Chapter 1

The Tadpole Trouble

Ellie's ears twitched at a soft, **wiggling** sound near the stream.

It wasn't a **buzz.** It wasn't a splash.

It was a gentle swishing sound.

Curious, Ellie crept closer to see what could be making it.

Ollie hurried eagerly up beside her.

In a **shallow** puddle near the edge of the stream, tiny black shapes wriggled through the water.

Ellie **gasped.** "Tadpoles!"

They **flicked** their little tails, swimming in tight circles.

Tiny **ripples** shimmered across the water.

"There are so many," whispered Ellie.

Meet Ellie, a clever ginger kitten, and Ollie, a wise golden retriever.

Together, they go on secret missions that no human must ever know.

Ellie & Ollie's mission
We promise to:
* Look for friends in trouble
* Be brave and kind
* Help when someone needs us
* Never give up
Signed. * ·Ellie – Ollie

Chapter 2

The Shrinking Water

"The water is getting lower," Ellie said, her voice filled with **worry**.

Ollie looked **closely** at the puddle.

The edges were drying. The water was slowly **disappearing** into the ground.

"They won't last long like this," he said gently.

Ellie **studied** the ground carefully.

Stones and dirt **blocked** the puddle from the nearby stream.

"If we move that," she said slowly, "the water might flow back in."

"A water path!" Ollie barked excitedly.

His tail **wagged** quickly as he looked at Ellie with bright, **hopeful** eyes.

Ellie smiled, feeling a little spark of hope.

They ran to Mission
Base.

Drawers opened.

Tools **clattered.**

"What can help us move
the rocks?" Ellie asked.

Ollie **carried** a sturdy stick in his mouth.

Ellie **wedged** it carefully under a small rock.

"Use it to lift," she said.

Together, they pushed down gently, slow and **steady.**

They knew every second mattered.

Chapter 3

The Flowing Stream

Ellie **nudged** one last
stone out of the way.

The water **suddenly** rushed forward in a thin, sparkling stream.

It **spilled** over the edge of the stones and into the puddle.

It **swirled** gently around the tadpoles.

The puddle grew **wider** and deeper.

The tadpoles **drifted** with the current toward the larger pool nearby.

"They're moving!" said Ellie.

Then a **shadow** glided beneath the water.

"Wait," Ollie said, his voice low.

A hungry fish swam slowly through the **deeper** pool.

It **circled** quietly beneath the surface of the water.

Its eyes watched the tiny, wriggling tadpoles.

Chapter 4

The Waiting Watch

Ellie stepped carefully into the shallow edge of the pool, her eyes fixed on the fish.

Tall reeds **swayed** gently around them in the breeze.

The water **rippled** softly across the surface.

The fish circled a little closer.

Ellie held her breath, her paws steady but tense.

The tadpoles **drifted** helplessly in the water.

They were unaware of the **danger** below.

The fish darted forward through the water.

Ollie stepped **quickly** into the stream with a splash.

Ripples spread out around them.

"Over here," Ollie said calmly, moving slowly to draw the fish away.

The fish turned, **curious**.

Ellie gently guided the tadpoles using her paw.

They moved toward the **shallower** edge using her paw.

The water swirled as they drifted in the right direction.

A breeze **stirred** gently
across the water.

The tadpoles **drifted**
away again with the
movement.

"Oh no," said Ellie.

Ollie **shifted** carefully, keeping himself between the fish and the tadpoles.

"This way," he **murmured**, guiding the fish further away.

The tadpoles gathered near the edge, where the water was **calmer** and safer.

Ellie watched them closely, her heart **pounding** with worry and hope.

33

Days passed.

The sun **warmed** the water.

Tiny changes began to happen.

Ellie blinked in **surprise.**
"Ollie... look!" she
whispered.

One tiny tadpole had
grown little legs.

It wiggled, then pushed
gently against the
water.

"This is the hardest part," Ollie said softly.

He watched the tiny frogs closely as they **bobbled** in the water.

"They're still very small," he added.

The tiny frog wobbled toward the edge.

It slipped slightly, then tried again.

Ellie leaned closer, ready to help.

Chapter 5

The First Leap

Sunlight shimmered across the water as the more of the tiny frogs reached the edge.

Ollie wagged his tail, his eyes **shining** with pride.

"They made it this far," he said gently.

"They're almost ready."

Ellie smiled **softly** as she watched them closely.

The tiny frogs wobbled safely near the edge of the water.

"They just needed a little help," she said.

The tiny frog gave a small, **wobbly** hop onto the soft ground.

Then another.

Then another.

They made it at last.

Mission Notes!

Another successful mission!
We worked together to
solve a problem.
We found useful tools.
We helped another creature.

Ellie's ears twitched again.

Somewhere in the garden...

Another adventure waited.

Ellie & Ollie's
GARDEN MISSION
CHECKLIST

Can you see tiny tadpoles
wriggling in the shallow water?
Can you spot them drifting
through the sparkling stream?
Is there a little creature nearby
that needs your gentle help
today?

Other secret missions:

Thank you for reading The Secret Adventures of Ellie and Ollie!

Connect with me on Instagram and share your reading journey.

You can also send your Ellie and Ollie artwork in to be considered to feature in their next adventure.

Schools and libraries can also request an author visit.